AF350660

<u>**Happy & Present in 2-minutes: A Practical Guide to Calm Your Mind, Thoughts & Feelings – With No Meditation.**</u>

(Mindfulness Guide)

Contents

Introduction

The Journey to Find Freedom

In this book you will discover how to attain one of the most powerful and satisfying experiences of life – **total acceptance** of life itself.

This is extremely valuable if you're someone who wants to combat stress and anxiety, things that have happened in your life, making it difficult to move on, or even if you just want to transform your life to a whole new level and experience life in a more fulfilling way.

The transformation I'm talking about is like going back to how you once were – as a kid. Where each moment was never consumed by the things that happened to you or things you had to do. Where your mind never worked against you, and each moment felt beautiful.

It's about eliminating the conditioning of the modern world, which will lead us back into our natural state, where each moment connects us to the experience of the present moment.

While it sounds mystical to many, this book will reveal to you a vivid, **PRACTICAL** and easy way to achieve it.

Within this book I will also share with you my newfound ability to change beliefs - **The QPH Method**.

The QPH Method is a combination of 3 powerful principles that are always working. It is an ability that you already have, which gives you power to take control of the very process of why your experience is the way that it is.

As you read the book, you'll discover that these principles are already proven and supported by the sciences of **Physics, Psychology and Physiology.**

And together, they provide an effective way to deal with the very source of all thoughts, emotions and experience of life – and how you see the world around you. Together, they give you an ability to control your subconscious mind, memory and beliefs, and achieve real change in a matter of days – _while making it last a lifetime._

As you read further you will find out exactly how it works and discover how your experience gets created in simplified principles. Once you learn what these principles are, you'll understand how me, and my students have used this method to achieve the most incredible transformations in our lives. And more importantly – <u>you will be able to do the same.</u>

The problem of our experience is that we have many things that prevent us from achieving happiness and presence in each moment of our lives.

Even if we're good for the most part, often our thoughts, emotions and considerations of our never-ending to-do list take over. Living in a modern busy world full of distraction, confusion, excessive stimulus and too much information.

It can become extremely hard to enjoy simple moments in our lives and relationships when worry, stress and anxiety takes over. And when things become good, often, we live with the habits we've developed, and sometimes they haunt us, preventing us from enjoying simple moments in life.

This was how I was led to discover the processes and principles of how this whole process we call life really works. *Which was the first key to changing it.*

Back in 2015 I was going through absolute hell inside of my mind. After I turned 19 and had to travel abroad to study Sports Medicine at the University of Aberdeen, Scotland, my childhood autoimmune disease followed me. And it felt like <u>it came back with a vengeance.</u>

My body degraded very quickly until I began to react to everything I ate. I couldn't even have a slice of bread without having my body turning against me. Every day I looked at my skin – turning red, like a reptile.

Every time I went to work, I looked at people, worried that they might see bandages underneath my clothes and how bad my skin looked. Every time I placed a glass on the table for customers, I watched their faces, thinking *'they can see me'*...

To keep this book short and on point - I was fortunate to eventually overcome my condition and go back to living a normal life.

Or at least I hoped that it would be like it was...

While the disease no longer affected my body, I came to find that <u>it had a hold over my mind.</u>

All of sudden ordinary experiences were full of worry, anxiety and weakness. I couldn't speak with people; I couldn't express myself with confidence - I couldn't feel comfortable. Talk about enjoying your life – my pain was consuming me...

I couldn't understand 'why I was feeling that way?'; 'Why was I anxious and different to how I once was?'

All I wanted was to get out of that daily cycle of negative thoughts, emotions, situations taking over my life every day.

As the only resort, I began to pick up books in my attempt to improve my condition. I've read over a 100 of books on Confidence and tried every single tip, trick, secret, exercise or practice the Experts preach.

Every time I tried something, I felt better, believing that 'maybe this time, I will find what really works'.

Every time I applied their techniques I saw better results, which improved how I felt – *at least for a while...*

Ever since I came back from a condition which completely consumed my life, I wasn't able to settle for anything but a complete solution to my problem. The more I wanted to fix it, the more I found myself back where I was. *Sometimes, even worse than before, I read books or applied their solutions.*

Eventually I stumbled on a book that would change everything. This one book was able to give me the one thing I needed in order to find the root cause of it all.

The book was called 'The Power of Positive Thinking' by Norman Vincent Peale (1898-1993), which gave me a consideration, that my mind and my thoughts may somehow play a part in creating my problems, pain and barriers that consumed me.

The next day, I went to work, I simply did what I did with all other advice – I tried and applied it.

I listened to each thought I was having.

Better yet, I listened to my thoughts in the midst of chaos and the life outside. Every time something happened. Every time I felt stress, pain or worry – *I observed.*

And what I found was that there are thoughts beneath the surface of our everyday thinking. The subconscious thoughts. That leave our minds as quickly as they come in.

And if you can catch them, you can begin to see the connection, how every single thought connect to the feeling you're about to feel.

Ever since I began to practice this, what I call – self-awareness, I realized, that the real problem was not what was happening outside of me – but how my mind and habits of thought were creating my perceptions, feelings and experience of life.

The Power of Self-Awareness

It was when I began to see **HOW my experience was being created** that I was free – <u>to gain power over it</u>. It was the ONE thing that allowed me to find a way on how to change my situation.

It was about the process happening inside my own body, that was dictating my life.

I've realized, people are fighting the wrong fight. They are facing the world the wrong way. Instead of understanding exactly how their life is being created from within, <u>they are looking at the things happening 'outside' of them.</u>

The real battleground is happening inside our minds. We carry it with us, we lay with it – we can't even sleep because of it.

Until I realized that it was my mind creating my lack of confidence – _I had no way to achieve it from the outside._ Maybe temporarily, but not indefinitely.

Most people live each day working on their lives and very few people are even aware that their mind is what creates each barrier between the life they want to live and the life they have right now.

If you go on YouTube, TikTok or read books, you will find advice like _'you have to value yourself'_ which sounds amazing but has no practical value or deliver any use that would help us fix our problems. You'll see them talking about grooming, body language, self-care or even escaping and going for a walk.

If these methods worked, why would mental health issues and conditions be rapidly increasing?

Every piece of advice given in books, courses or by experts is focused not on the process that is going on in our minds but fixing and sorting the 'life outside'.

Why? Because no one knows – that you can actually control the deeper parts of your mind. The very bits that dictate what thoughts come up in your mind, what feelings arise, and how you are moved to act.

What you'll find in this short book will be a series of principles that I was led to discover. Each principle was like a steppingstone towards understanding how life experience gets created through our minds.

This is what led me to pioneer an ability, through which I was able to change that experience and my entire life in a matter of days.

Ever since then I've built a maximum level of confidence in how I see myself, in the things I do. To this day I carry the qualities that I've programmed into my mind everywhere I go, and my mind can never make me weak again. Being able to turn my whole life around like that was the greatest thing in life.

While most people need to escape life through practice of meditation, or just to run away from chaos – I can enjoy it in the midst of it all.

If I take a bus, my mind can never wander to the future thinking about what I need to buy for groceries, or go to the past, being consumed by what happened at work, who did what or said what.

It's always present.

While it may sound spiritual – remember your childhood. Everything you did was beautiful and exciting. You could sit in a tree and do nothing, and it felt amazing. You could be with your friends, playing and each moment was thrilling and wholesome.

As we grow up, figure out how life works and get conditioned how to live in it – we lose that sense of wholeness.

We begin to live our lives consumed by our thoughts, overwhelmed by emotions. Things we need to do, situations we need to consider, pains we need to deal with. The further we move into modern society, the more confused, distracted and overwhelmed we get.

With labels of ADHD, compulsive disorders, mental health rooms being built in the world, it's apparent – life right now is quickly getting worse.

We don't have the luxury of hopeful thinking 'one day I will arrive', 'One day I can rest' and 'One day I'll have enough'.

What I'm talking about is not mystical – it's NATURAL. It's how you were made to live your life.

With this book is my goal to show you how through reconditioning the mind from all the barriers that get created you can go back to that and bring that balance back into your life.

To help you achieve that, I feel the duty and desire to share with you what I consider to be the most powerful human ability.

Unlike other methods that focus on changing things outside of us, it is a practical approach that deals with the very source of our experience – inside of our minds, which creates the world we live outside. The only way you can begin to see a complete and permanent transformation in your life.

And I want to share with you things that I find extremely valuable – principles. Because principles are something that are always present. They explain **why things work the way they do.**

When you acquire a principle, and you use it or apply it with other people - you can't help but see it work again. Because you know WHY it works.

Each lesson I share with you in these chapters will be a powerful principle, that once you learn you'll begin to see it all around you. Once you experience it you will begin to see the value that it has.

Once you see it, experience it – you will understand *why life is the way that it is.*

Chapter 1 – The WHY of Your Experience

There's nothing more important than understanding **WHY things work the way they do.**

When you are little and you want to ride a bike, it is only when you understand how it works that you are capable of getting on it and riding it.

Imagine, I put you in an alien ship, you've never seen before, and give you the controls, with dozens of buttons, levers and screens and say – fly it.

You would instantly get lost.

This is the reason why most people end up dealing with the symptoms of their problems, without understanding why their symptoms appeared in the first place.

The concept of the 'Inside world' explains why most people can't find things they want to have, because they are not aware <u>that they simply might come from a different place.</u>

In this chapter, my goal is to reveal to you the simple principles of why your life works the way it does. How it is directly linked with the life you're having 'outside'. How the very process that happens inside your body creates the entirety of your inside & outside world. And how you can gain a new level of control and freedom in your life.

So, let's have a look at - <u>how it all works.</u>

The Focus of The Mind: One Wrong Belief

Inside of your mind you have a mechanism so powerful that is saving your life and keeping you alive this very minute.

It's called – **The Reticular Activation System (RAS).**

RAS sits deep inside our brains, at the very center where it connects with the spinal cord. Where our mind connects with our body.

What is important about it is - <u>its function.</u> Because it holds ALL of the power over your life. And when you can begin to control it – *you will have power over your life.*

The Reticular Activation System's job is to help you **<u>survive</u>**. And the way it does it, is by bringing everything you believe – into your focus. <u>*Into your life.*</u>

Reticular Activation System works in a way where your mind only see's what you believe - while eliminating everything else from your focus and awareness.

It acts like Google - whatever you enter into the search results – is exactly what you get. When you type in 'Weight loss for Adults' it doesn't show you 'how to become a millionaire'. It shows you exactly what you search for.

The reason why it does that is to show you the world you know. Because the only way you can survive in the world – <u>is if you know how the world works.</u>

Meaning that your mind is constantly seeking certainty and familiarity. And what is familiar to you are the things you learn and experience:

<u>Your beliefs</u> and **<u>your memories</u>** *(associated feelings of experience).*

For example, if a woman loses her baby in a big crowd, her mind will go into survival mode and it will begin to focus only on the voice of her child, the clothes that he was wearing and specific features that he has, eliminating everything else. She will almost be able to hear 1 voice, amid 1000 other sounds being heard in the moment.

A person who believes he is 'unworthy' will only see himself have experiences of low self-worth, even if you tell him something positive.

This mechanism is powerful beyond belief, and it controls what our minds are open to experience.

While it may seem like the greatest gift, which gives us an ability to survive and experience the pleasures of life – it is also our greatest *weakness*.

The basic premise of this is that at the very core – **it is our beliefs, and past memories** that create every single thought, feeling and action we feel. Allow me to illustrate it:

Imagine Jack – an 8-year-old boy, who is going with his cousin Jimmy to the beach. His cousin is a few years older, and he happened to put some money aside over time. So, he thinks it would be pretty nice to buy some candy to enjoy the sunny day with his little causing who came to visit. And have a nice experience.

They both go out, have a swim at the beach and on their way back, they're talking about playing some games online for the rest of their evening. And because Jimmy had some money, he said we could get some candy for the occasion.

They go to a small shop close to home, Jimmy buys the candy, comes out and gives half of it to Jack. They both head home in full arms of sweets, feeling excited.

As they walk, their grandmother sees them, looking through the window of the top floor flat. Which she always does, just to observe life happening outside, as she's too old to take long walks.

Right before Jack and Jimmy ring the doorbell, they hide their candy in their jackets, so that their sisters don't see and feel bad about it. But the moment they walk through the doorstep of their home, their parents immediately say 'empty your pockets'.

As they are in a dead-end, they take out all the candy they bought. And their parents take ALL of it away. On top of that they get punished, that it's very bad that they bought all the candy for themselves and didn't get anything for the girls. Their parents simply wanted to teach them a lesson to share.

Now they're confused. In their mind, they didn't do anything bad – 'it was our own money'. If the girls wanted to buy candy, they could just use their savings... They feel bad, unjust and their whole idea for the evening is ruined.

(It may just seem like an ordinary experience.)

20 years later, Jack is thinking of writing a book. He has a brand-new idea and thinks it would be pretty cool to share it with the world. So, as he begins to write a book, he finds other cool stuff and upgrades his idea.

He puts everything in the book. In his mind this book just became something he didn't even expect it to be. He thinks this is my idea and it's valuable beyond anything I could imagine.

But suddenly, his mind starts to wander... 'But, what if I lose it though?'... 'What if something happens to me, and nobody will find this new idea?'... *his heart begins to race, he notices the beats of his heart...* 'what if my heart stops and I get a heart attack?'...

For weeks on end, he can't go on with continuing with the book. All he is thinking about the worst-case scenarios... obsessing, worrying what might happen? What might not happen?...

Until one day, he couldn't handle it anymore and said to himself 'I can't lose it...'.

'I'm going to send a copy to my sister and my friend, give them my passwords and tell them, if anything happens to me – please finish the job for me.'.

He told his friends that he's feeling anxious, and it would be great if they could help him. After that he felt at ease and was able to continue with the book.

(That's it, problem over...)

Now, could you see where the Reticular Activation System took hold of Jack's life?

Let me show you.

20 years later, Jack didn't think about what happened when he was little. Yet if he had to remember the things that happened during his early days – he would be able to recall that experience. Maybe with some effort – but eventually he would remember.

Most of the things we remember are emotionally charged experiences, that become our memories. You do not remember a random evening 12 years, 158 days and 16 hours ago... You remember things that through emotion, get saved in your mind.

That memory 20 years ago created an association in Jacks mind – that 'it is painful, to lose what you have'.

He felt intense emotions as he had to give all his excitement and joy of having so much candy. Those emotions of pain became a new association, a belief – of 'how painful it is to lose something'.

Now 20 years later, everything looks different. New time, new place, new people – even new Jack. Everything is different. But the moment there was a potential that Jack might lose something he had – the emotions of pain came back.

His mind was warning him of potential pain – and he began to worry, stress out, think and feel – focusing and seeing only the negative side of things.

His Reticular Activation System kicked into high gear:

1st, it was showing him the pain to move away from – so that he could survive.

2nd, it proved to him that in fact – it is painful to lose something.

In other words, his mind *showed him* his belief and – it became his reality.

You see the Reticular Activation System is so powerful that it will show you exactly what you believe – and you won't be able to see the opposite.

A million years ago, when a tiger attacked you – you would only focus on potential danger, and completely neglect the apple you might have been picking.

You would not be thinking about the pleasure of eating an apple, you would not be thinking about how nice it would be to have two and bring one for your loved one. Nothing but complete focus on **pain – <u>survival.</u>**

It highlights that <u>negative emotion which is part of fear – is way more powerful than good emotions.</u> Because it helps us survive. It pushes us away from what we believe can cause us pain or kill us.

Even though in Jacks example, he was in no real danger – his mind can't distinguish that. Pain is there to guide us in life, so that if we burn once – we avoid doing it again.

RAS helps us predict these moments. As we begin to focus on the possible outcome of pain, <u>that's all we see.</u>

The more we focus -> the more we see -> the more emotions build up –> *pushing us stronger and stronger.*

We put energy in ONE place and make it **grow**.

You see Jack had no control over how his Parents will punish him. Even his Parents didn't have control – because everything they got – was also from their parents...

Maybe Jack could've gone through writing his book with breeze, confidence, courage and fulfillment if he had not had <u>that one thing</u> happen to him in his life – which created that experience and that memory *(belief of how something feels)* in his mind.

<u>But why was Jack able to keep going? Why was he able to move on and forget about this 'random' moment in his life?</u>

Well, our minds and our bodies are designed by some powerful laws of nature (which you'll learn in a bit). Which is why this mechanism has a weakness...

The problem with this mechanism is that it brings into our reality everything we believe – good and bad.

So, let's say your mind is focusing on 'not having confidence', that it's painful to be weak and feel weak – showing you the worst-case scenarios in potential situations and creating pain so that you move away from them... This time a memory/belief is not about something on the outside, it's about something you always carry with you – **<u>your IDENTITY</u>**.

What would happen if you kept focusing, thinking, obsessing over something?

You probably guessed it – you would be feeling worse and worse. And if your mind would do that without a stop - you wouldn't want to live anymore OR your body would get physically sick from all the stress and pain, destroying it from inside-out.

<u>That's why your first survival mechanism needs a second survival mechanism - to counter this effect.</u>

The Power of Focus:

There's something extremely powerful about the power of focusing your attention onto something.

A group of Psychologist Researchers did a famous experiment, where they've illustrated the power of Belief, Reticular Activation System and Focus.

After gathering a room of people for the test, they instructed everyone to look for a color (say **blue**) and count how many times they've found it in the room and write it down.

After that, they told the participants to look for a different color (say **brown**) and count how many times they've found it and write it down.

Then they told the participants to go back to the first color (**blue**) and again count how many times they've found it and write it down.

What they found was that the second time people looked for color blue, the participants found significantly more blue than the first time.

The problem was, they found way more blue, than there actually was in the room. On top of that, the first time they had enough time to find all of the blue colors.

So how were they able to find more of the color?

What they found was that participants began to see all colors close enough to blue, as blue. They began to identify relative colors, as blue.

Which led to identify, that when the mind focuses to find something – **it can find it even if it's not there.**

Whatever you focus on – _you find_. The more you focus on something, the more of it you find. *(Even if it's not there)*

A real-life illustration of this powerful example is, when a guy in a relationship feels insecure - he begins to focus on the pain and potential of 'losing his girlfriend'. The more he focuses on, the more he begins to see examples, where he may in fact 'lose her'. He begins to perceive the ordinary situations, that she may be cheating or enjoying the presence of another man too much. The more examples his mind finds – the more real it feels.

Even if it's not true... (The mind cannot distinguish, between what is real, and what we merely think about)

The Proccess Of Creation

What Keeps Us in the Loop and Takes Over Our Minds?

This is our second survival mechanism, which is powerful beyond belief. It helps us find a way out of pain and helps us escape fear.

It is **the Rational Mind**. Another mechanism deep inside our minds, but more specifically in the part which controls our modern ability – <u>thinking.</u>

You see with the first mechanism we would act like animals – simply moving from pain to pleasure. If we experience pain when a dog bites us, next time we might try to predict it, feel pain, react and fight to survive.

But the moment we've developed our ability to think consciously, to remember and to recall experiences into our conscious mind – we have a potential, that <u>our negative memories could begin to consume our thoughts and emotions in a negative way.</u>

That's why **we need the Rational Mind**. The purpose of rational mind is to find a **<u>Reason</u>**, to neutralize the pain coming from our thoughts and emotions.

By doing that our minds will always be able to avoid pain and fear getting out of control and causing us too much harm from excessively *seeing it, thinking about it and feeling it.*

Let's go back to Jack & Jimmys illustration. Remember when Jack first had his candy and sweets taken away? It must've felt painful right?

That's why initially he started thinking - <u>'We didn't do anything bad...'.</u>

And the second time, his RAS made him re-experience that same belief when he was writing a book his mind began to rationalize that negative feeling, trying to find a reason – <u>'What if I lose the book?', 'what if something happens to me?', 'I can't lose it...'.</u>

The mind is trying very hard to find a reason to make things okay, so that's when the thinking spirals out – until we find a reason/solution.

When he finally had **a reason** – his mind calms down and can move on – in balance.

In other words, rational mind provides balance, by neutralizing the emotions of pain and fear.

Often, we blame, find reasons creating new beliefs. This is the purpose of the Rational Mind. To bring the body and the mind back into balance. To connect one belief with another in our mind – _create a reason._

The Rational mind can keep our beliefs from ever changing. Preventing us from changing the belief – that caused that pain in the first place.

The point is that facing our thoughts head on and finding reasons is not going to help. Because we'll only be able to move on and still live with the same experiences coming from our beliefs and past associations.

The biggest problem is that we don't see the very mechanism, how we create pain, fear and conditions in our lives.

And this is where the third piece and a powerful principle of the brain comes into play.

The Loophole of The Mind: Cause of All Pain

When you understand this principle, on the other side of it you will find the most powerful dynamic in the Universe. _One which creates either chaos – **or peace.**_

As you can begin to realize, the mind holds a lot of power over our daily lives.

1. The RAS projects our beliefs and realities and controls what comes through to us from the outside world.
2. The Rational Mind always maintains that RAS doesn't focus only on pain and finds reasons to escape it (making us see our realities, think, feel and react to the 'world outside').

But there's a natural function of our brain, which creates all human misery, problems, pain – and initiates the processes of RAS and Rational mind, to spiral in a negative way.

(On the other side of which lies the answer of total acceptance, and **freedom)**

I was only able to find and understand this principle, when I was trying to understand – '**<u>what is fear?</u>**' And 'how does it work?'.

So, let's cover it quickly because fear and even pain, can be viewed in a very simple way.

First let's agree on one thing. <u>You can't be afraid of something, if it's not there.</u>

For example, if you believe a spider is dangerous, you can't feel the feeling of fear, if there's no spider, right?

It is only when the spider is there that you begin to feel fear. When the spider is there, you begin to resist that experience – ***you want it to be different.***

(That the spider wouldn't be there...)

Many people call this experience of pain and fear rising as **resistance**. What is resistance then?

It is - wanting for the moment to be different than the way it is. So, fear is when <u>you want the moment to be different</u>, so that the <u>thing you believe may cause you pain</u> – wouldn't harm you.

And that's where the principle of the brain comes in.

'Your brain can never work in the future or the past. <u>It always feeds back into the present moment.</u>'

What that means is that you can think ABOUT the future and ABOUT the past. But every thought you have travels into your mind and gets reflected to what you hold - in the moment. So that it can determine, based on all your beliefs – **HOW you can best survive.**

This is where the loophole connects with resistance, pain, stress, anxiety and fear.

Every time you WANT the present moment to be different than the way it is – it shows you how you DON'T HAVE it different right now.

For example, when you want the spider to not be there, it goes back into the present moment and shows you – that it is there. Creating pain to help you survive.

It is a principle function of the Reticular Activation System. You begin to focus on potential danger and the present moment.

If I say I want to be confident, my mind feeds back into the present moment re-affirming, that 'I'm not confident right now'. And directing the focus (RAS) on – seeing how insecure I am. Bringing more of it into my reality.

And when it becomes a habit of thought – it can become a belief.

When people want money because they don't have enough, their mind constantly goes into the present moment and shows them how they don't have it right now. Causing pain. Looking for reasons. Creating new beliefs, based on the previous beliefs.

When people get depressed and want to hold on to the idea of the person they lost, their mind goes into the present moment and shows them what they don't have this moment. Over time getting worse and, in many cases – *a lasting condition.*

This is how the brain naturally creates pain, fear, resistance and leads to rational mind bringing in thoughts trying to make sense of these negative situations.

But every time we make things okay, we keep getting back to the same place where the same experiences come back, and we see and feel those emotions once more.

The more we stuff something away the more it keeps coming back.

This is because Rational Mind Needs to make complete sense out of the negative experience – **and create a new belief** *(neutralizing connection).*

And the reason why we get these desires, experiences of pain, fear, resistance or anything negative – is because of our experience of the past - **<u>our beliefs.</u>**

Meaning our beliefs, thoughts, feelings, desires - create new beliefs, based on the previous beliefs.

For example, if you believe you're not confident –> you want to be confident. Every time you want to be confident -> the mind travels into the present moment and with the power of RAS

(Focus) keeps showing you where in fact you find yourself – not confident.

Each experience becomes evidence for the belief –> that in fact, the belief is true (real). And when you see yourself that way -> you feel bad. And when you feel bad -> you begin to look for reasons. And you come up with a new belief –> 'maybe I'm an introvert'.

It's ONLY when you change your sponsoring belief – that the whole cycle can change. It's when you fix the problem, at the very source of where it is being created, that you can change your entire experience. For example:

When you believe '**you are confident**', with the power of RAS and focus you begin to see experiences and moments, where in fact you find yourself confident (this moment). Each experience gives feelings and experience, which re-affirm in your mind that the belief in fact – is true (real). And because you believe you're confident, you feel confident. And because you feel confident – you cannot want what you already have.

Rule of Life (Physics) – Universal Law of Polarity

According to Science, everything in the world is created by **energy**.

Whether mental or physical, all scientists agree that we are made of energy and everything in the world is created by energy.

Universal Laws are like Gravity. You can't deny it, it exists – every single moment in time. They're always present.

Our minds and our lives are constantly being created through these natural laws. And The Universal Law of Polarity is one of the most influential laws in our lives.

The Law of Polarity says – everything has two sides. <u>You cannot have one without the other.</u>

For example – without white, you wouldn't know what black means. Without pain, you wouldn't know what pleasure means.

When you focus on pain – you cannot feel pleasure. You can only have one, at one moment in time. This is why, when people feel negative emotions, and they focus on them – they can't feel good. The more they focus on the negative – *the more negative energy grows.*

When you believe you are not confident – you cannot believe you are confident.

But when you change a negative belief or association about something in your mind – <u>your mind can no longer create the negative.</u>

Because on a spectrum of good and bad, you can only have one or the other. **<u>Not BOTH.</u>**

Love and fear can't happen in one moment. If you focus on love, it grows. You see more of it, feel more of it, believe you have it.

When you focus on pain, you see more of it, feel more of it, believe you WANT to get what's on the other side.

The Cause of Emotional Confusion

The Law of Polarity gives us a better understanding of all emotional intelligence there is.

The world has made it a complicated science, where we have an *infinite number of <u>different emotions.</u>*

Every emotion feels different, every emotion is named different – and the more we divide them, the more confused we get what they are and what they mean.

In biology and by evolution, our bodies come from an animal world. And in the animal world, while a dog can experience loss and grief, what they really feel is one emotion – **pain**.

Everything that excites them, makes them happy, thrilled, initiates pleasure – leads to **pleasure**.

In reality there are only two emotions – fear and love. Pain and pleasure. Good and bad. Positive and negative.

Only TWO sides. The rest - we have created.

We have created labels for themes where similar situations re-occur, like when we appear worse than others we call it **shame**, if we do something wrong, we call it **guilt**, if we lose someone, we call it **grief**.

Our emotions have the same biological resemblance like an animal one. They are designed to help us <u>survive</u>.

When we feel PAIN (or any negative emotion) – <u>we move away from it.</u> When we predict feeling pain, we feel more pain, growing, trying to warn us of danger.

When we feel pain at a high enough level, we feel that we can't handle it – we call it **fear**.

When we feel PLEASURE (or any positive emotion) – <u>we want to move toward it.</u>

The same like any animal, we come from the same world, and part of our brain responds to these emotions without thinking.

If you want to confuse a person to no end and make sure he doesn't understand something, you apply the principle *'divide and conquer'*. The more different labels you create, the more the person is lost between division. The more people are lost – the easier it is to gain power over him.

(Whether it's done consciously or naturally in our world, let's leave it for another time.)

What you will find that when you begin to look at your life from a perspective that everything is an ASSOCIATION of the past, the things you've learned to feel <u>pleasureful</u> or <u>painful</u>, that dictate your thoughts and perceptions, you can begin to track down why you feel the way you do in the first place.

Look for when was the first time you've experienced pain in a similar situation and find the ROOTS of when was the first memory, the first belief created.

AUTOMATIC NEEDS   BELIEFS

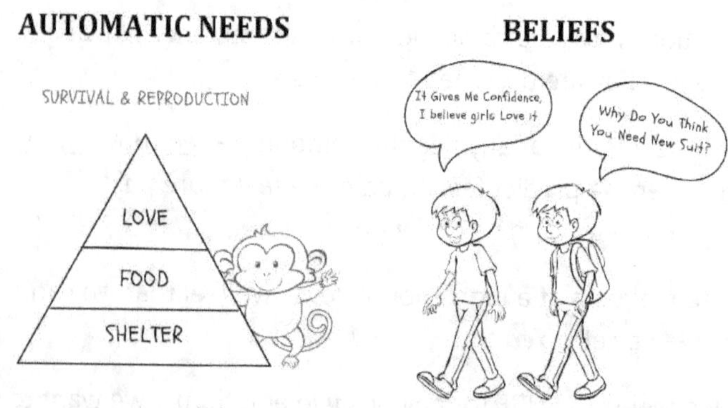

The Root Cause of All Confusion

The first problem is that we hold a belief in our minds that the world is 'outside of us'. That reality and the things happening 'outside of us' is what makes us feel.

But what about two people who can have the same experience, but experience it in an entirely different way? When one person jumps off plain with a parachute, he can feel excitement, while another – stress, fear and anxiety.

It is our minds and our beliefs – how we perceive the world, what we find pleasurable and what we find painful, that creates our reality.

After we are born, we are taught by our parents that life is 'outside of us'. We get told what is what, and what means what. We learn the consequences of our actions in the outside world. And we develop a perspective of - *reality*.

We learn to always face 'outside'.

Our parents never sit down with us to teach us how to introspect, how to examine our thinking, how to question things, how our thoughts get created and what our feelings mean. We don't look at anything that happens within us.

Because we always face outside, our Reticular Activation System projects this perception into REALITY.

It's like a global consensus. When you look around, you will find all around you how people who want to improve their confidence are being told that they need to change their body language, say the right pickup-line, improve their voice projection, fake it till they make it and so on. Every single thing is outside of them – and people keep searching, tip after tip, hack after hack. Looking for that golden secret of how to create something inside, through the outside world.

People are looking for love, fulfilment, self-confidence, self-esteem, happiness, presence in places – <u>where it can never be found.</u>

This is what I don't like about 98% of self-help and self-development industry – people end up treating the symptoms, rather than having a cure *(without even knowing)*.

First you had the Science of Psychology which accurately found the roots of most human experiences.

And if you attempted to change the perception of your past experience – you would change how you feel in the future.

The problem is that there is no way to really take past experience and completely resolve it. Instead, it takes years of time, you have to go see someone and share your darkest experiences with and pay a hefty fee of $100 to $1000's on a continuous basis. For many people amounting up to $50,000 a year, to do deep work. In the end merely changing your perspective.

The best part about The QPH Method, and the ability to change beliefs, is that you can change the entire experience of the past and present, resolve it in a matter of days and at the privacy of your own mind. And make it permanent. Showing the way how real change was meant to be.

This is how I was able to go from having my childhood affect my future feelings of <u>loss</u> and <u>rejection</u> to having complete freedom, save my future relationships, and be able to approach people and express myself with complete self-comfort. Naturally being able to say what I think, and express how I feel.

I even went from being bankrupt, in debt $9k and owing $2k to my first girlfriend, to start making $2k/day. Eliminating all barriers that were preventing me from seeing how money really works and how easy it is to earn it.

It's because when you change how you experience the world – what you get out of life changes.

But then the world changed and they introduced CBT where you treat 'life outside' in order to change how you 'feel inside' so that you can move on. *Which is like a band aid.*

The goal becomes to make you feel better by focusing on different things and areas in your life. Changing your perspective, talking out and releasing the negativity.

While it may FEEL beneficial to rationalize the thoughts and release your emotions when you talk things out, the problem is that *it's a temporary band aid.*

You improve your situation – without fixing it completely. Only to allow you to move on with life. Again, this creates a constant need for the service, so you keep coming back when things come after you, when problems re-occur, and when you want to feel good again.

The biggest problem I have with this is that I was coping with my situation for several years, living in bandages, suffering with the consequences of my autoimmune disease. And coping never fixed the problem. Feeling better and being able to prolong life was not the way.

I didn't want to settle with coping, improving or taking a sedative pill. I wanted to change it <u>once and for all</u>. And I want to make sure that you wouldn't have to settle for it either.

<u>We have to realize that this is a problem.</u> The modern world we live in today is already full of opportunities to escape our problems and distract ourselves with something else.

100 years back, if you had a problem, you were alone with it. If you had to go see your neighbor, it could take you hours just to see them for a short while. You were left with your mind, <u>for most of the time.</u>

On top of that, people were not as close, relationships were supported by strong family households, where family name meant something, and men and women hadn't yet turned against each other.

The problems we faced weren't reflected back to us on a constant basis. We didn't see people as much, we didn't have the internet, we didn't compare ourselves as easily.

Everything around us is designed in a way that it would be easy and appealing to choose the escape. Everything is designed with an appeal to our animal brain, to bring pleasure fast and easy.

The further we moved away from nature, into a complex world of too much stimulus, too much information, people and situations happening all around us – the more it affected these imbalances, beliefs and conditions in our minds. Our weaknesses and beliefs get reflected back to us a 1000-fold.

We have more practice, more access to knowledge, more information, more development, but mental health problems are higher than they ever were. Anxiety, social anxiety, fears, ADHD, compulsive disorders became a common experience. We are literally building mental health rooms in workplaces in the world, so that people can escape.

When you combine it with food that is filled with sensitive hormones (estrogen), so that food would grow faster, absorb energy faster and we begin to consume it, the more we became vulnerable to these experiences and occurrences.

Estrogen, when it begins to dominate our natural hormones in the body, can slow our bodies down, as they become <u>too sensitive.</u> When our bodies slow down and become sensitive, we feel things more intense. Stress hormones affect us stronger. All of which influences chemicals in our brains (neurotransmitters), making our brains activate thoughts, coming from survival. Thoughts of worry and insecurity. This means thoughts of perceiving danger, insecurity, worry, stress only become easier to experience and more frequent.

This is what gives rise to panic attacks – when belief creates a trigger experience – but the body feels it to an extreme and goes into <u>full survival mode</u> (*loss of control – fear, uncertainty*).

Everything that I'm revealing to you in this book, one important fact to understand is that while the root cause starts at the mind – **<u>the body affects the mind.</u>**

50% of all of our experiences come from how we feel physically, while the other 50% comes from how we perceive the world, think and feel about it. And while the mind affects the hormones, the feelings and the chemicals in your body – the food we eat and the chemicals we create in our body, *affect the functions of our mind.*

Most people don't notice what effect food has on their body, because it requires <u>a skill of awareness</u>. Mind-to-Experience and Body-to-Experience connection awareness is what mindfulness, the practice of self-awareness and self-discovery is all about. These are the practices of world's most wisdomous people, from ancient philosophers to Monks and Yogis who live in the mountains today.

I was blessed to have developed an extreme self-awareness, because I have an allergy to black pepper and vanilla... My throat swells from eating any restaurant meal, including most bakery and sweet things...

It was one hell of a ride to find out what caused my suffering. For years, with every meal – I trained to observe objectively. Combine it with my studies of Advanced Psychology, Sports Medicine and nutrition it gave me an ability to see and understand how food works and affects our body, our mind and our experience at a whole different level.

But the essential point I'm making – <u>the more we move away from nature, the worse we are getting.</u> That the way you combat this world of confusion, is by gaining a skill of awareness, control of your mind and acquire knowledge how your 'inside world' connects with the world outside. Have your mind open to the right information.

Our minds and this one wrong belief – that the world is 'out there', is what prevents us from finding out why we fight in relationships, why we get feelings of jealousy, why we lack **self**-esteem or **self**-confidence, courage, **self**-sufficiency, why we have money barriers, why we end up in overdraft each month unable to get back on track. Trying to change our reality and experience from outside-in, rather than from inside-out.

This is the power of belief. <u>It can either show us the way, or blind us from it.</u>

Rule of Life: Universal Law of Attraction

This is another universal law, like gravity. And many people have learned the power of it, but not in the way they can control it.

The Law of Attraction states that energy attracts energy. Because it's always *in-motion*. That you're like a magnet taking in energy from food and outside and transforming it into outcomes outside of you.

For example, when you hold the thoughts of love in your mind – you experience love in your reality. You bring experiences and things outside of you, into your reality.

This was popularized by famous books 'The Secret' by Rhonda Byrne and 'Think and Grow Rich' by Napoleon Hill who studied under Thomas Edison, and interviewed world's most successful people, wanting to see what brought them their greatest success in life.

The problem after people discovered the power of thinking we have in our lives is that people attributed that energy is created - **_by our thinking._**

People began to practice thought exercises – like visualization, saying affirmations to <u>change their thinking</u>, practice of positive thinking and changing their thoughts through workbooks and exercises.

It became a new science and a magical wonder – that if you THINK you have something – you will bring it into your reality.

Now while this law is always present and absolute, the mistake that was made is that it isn't thoughts that create our reality.

Yes, it is a fact that if you change a negative thought, to a positive thought – you will change a negative feeling, into a positive feeling.

But as we covered the principles of the mind and how your brain works, now it can become apparent – that doesn't matter how much you try to change your thinking, it is your beliefs that create your thoughts and your reality.

And even if you change your thinking, and feel better, and believe it works – it does no good, if you have beliefs that act like barriers, that block you from seeing and taking opportunities. If they block you from taking action. If they self-cultivate new beliefs, through desire, lack and rationalization.

But if you look at beliefs, you will find that <u>this law is always in effect.</u> If you believe a spider can cause you harm and you see a spider, you in effect – ATTRACT that belief into your reality.

If you believe you don't have confidence and your mind focuses on showing you that belief being real – everywhere you go you will find experiences coming into your life – where in fact, that belief becomes REAL.

You are the creator of your life - with every perception, thought, feeling, word and action you create your reality. But at the very root, it is not our thoughts that make our world – it is our beliefs.

And if you can change your beliefs, change the experiences of your past – you can change the experiences you will bring into your life in the future.

And indeed – <u>get what you desire.</u>

The first step is eliminating those blocks and barriers, which control *what you get* – and *what you don't get in life.*

How Our Minds Work Against Us?

Another thing is – people don't want to look inside. It's almost like their minds try very hard not to look inside and we want to get away from ourselves. Why?

Because a lot of associations and beliefs we naturally hold reveal our weaknesses and <u>hold our greatest pain.</u>

Even believing that we have a weakness can be painful...

People don't like trying to make sense of negative emotions. They don't like it when their mind starts thinking about the negative feelings and to take responsibility for them.

When someone experiences a breakup – he doesn't want to feel pain. He doesn't want to dive deep and understand himself. He wants to escape - go out and drink. Speak with someone. Runaway into a movie and unhealthy food. Sleep with someone else. Just not make sense of his or her emotions. **They don't want to be at fault** – they want to hear other people's opinions how the other person was at fault...

RAS will move us away from this 'inside world' reality, where we can experience pain, where we may just have to take responsibility, that we are somehow responsible for how we feel.

Protecting our minds from all the pain that hides inside, our minds happily show us that the outside world is to blame.

Dan Milman who attributed lessons of such magnitude to him winning an Olympic medal AFTER shattering his leg to pieces, said a powerful quote *(which is expressed in his book and movie 'The Way of A Peaceful Warrior'):*

> *'I want you to stop gathering information from outside yourself and start gathering from the inside. People are afraid of what's inside. And that's the only place they'll ever going to find what they need.'. - Socrates*

It becomes extremely easy for us to accept the reality that we are only at the effect of the world, giving away all responsibility to the 'outside world'.

We begin to rationalize everything that happens outside of us, we look for things to do outside of us, hoping to one day arrive.

Yet most people only realize at the end of life, when they let go of all the irrational fears and beliefs they hold for their entire lives – that it wasn't worth holding on to their beliefs and fears. And how much they lost because they allowed them to hold them from doing and having what they really wanted.

It is only when they accept their biggest fear – **the fear of death** (*survival*), that they are able to let go, of everything that was holding them and preventing them from doing and having what they really wanted.

So far, we've covered only a few powerful principles that make up our experience. In this short book I intend to give you the principles that are the most important to achieve a specific outcome – awareness, and ability to use The QPH Method to acquire happiness and presence.

I highly recommend that you read my full book with all concepts and principles - **'The QPH Method'**, a 300 page version.

There you'll find more powerful principles and gain better understanding of these principles and how they apply to EVERYTHING we experience.

On top of that you'll find way cooler ways on how to apply and leverage The QPH Method and these principles into your life. But for now, let's continue.

By now we've covered the core principles and perceptions that you need to have in order to be able to see how your experience is being created. You can probably notice and relate your experience in life with many of these principles.

If you experience anything negative in your life or even in occurrences, the coolest part of it all is that you can take this process and gain control over it. That's when it becomes your greatest gift.

And even if everything is going good enough in your life – when you gain control of this cycle, you can find peace and happiness from within, on a whole new level.

Remember this whole system and the power of our beliefs can be <u>our greatest gift</u> or <u>our greatest curse</u>.

So, how do we turn it all around? How do we gain control of this process creating our beliefs and our lives?

Chapter 2 – The KEY to Change Your Experience

Okay, so by now you may understand that what causes for our experience to be the way it is, are the thoughts and feelings –

which come from our **beliefs** and **associations** <u>about ourselves</u> or <u>the world</u>.

While Reticular Activation System is constantly showing you the reality of every belief, the Rational Mind jumps in to maintain balance.

Creating constant stream of thoughts and perceptions, creating our feelings which moves us to say things or act.

So, what do you do in order to control your mind? Be able to calm it? Change your beliefs and in effect – change your feelings?

The first time I found the answer on how to change beliefs, I had to really understand resistance and the principles that I've already laid down for you.

Remember, resistance is what makes us overthink things. When we stuff our feelings away, run from them or even try to shut ourselves off from them – they are left in our memory without meaning.

Our brains hold beliefs like a super-web. Every belief is connected with each other.

For example, if your beliefs create low self-worth, and you have several experiences where people treat you the way you see yourself and you experience that – you can rationalize that into a new belief - of being an introvert.

Now that belief is in alignment with all previous beliefs that would naturally lead you down this path. But it is connected and supported by how you feel and think about yourself.

When people get consumed by their thoughts or emotions – is when it wasn't fully and completely made sense out of. Is when people run from themselves, their thoughts and emotions.

It's when they avoid 'looking inside', and 'look outside' for a quick fix. That's when thoughts and feelings come back.

But the goal is not to make sense out of everything. The goal is not to sit down and find a reason for everything that your mind would simply stop thinking or overthinking. Why?

Because this way, it would simply be a band aid allowing you to move on. If you had a belief or perception which creates pain, and you create a new belief from rationalizing negative emotions – you will simply have another negative belief.

From having low self-esteem, to being in introvert, to avoiding people all together and buying cats as means of company and growing old without a partner is not the solution.

The circumstances would change – but the experiences would keep coming back, by your beliefs bringing them into your reality. This is still coping with life and taking what life gives you.

Instead, you want to create your life the way you want it to be. Have the experiences you want. Create your self-image which would give you a life of your dreams.

How do you do that? **By changing your beliefs.**

How do you change your beliefs? By applying one of the laws from previous chapter to pain, resistance and fear.

Resistance is wanting for something to be different than the way it is. The more you WANT something – the more you see how you don't have it. Focusing on your desires therefore <u>fuels the lack of what we want.</u>

But when you apply **The Law of Polarity**, and begin to focus on having what you want, instead of wanting – you'll begin to see how you HAVE the very thing you want. And if you remember how Focus works – <u>you will get it even if it's not there yet...</u>

The first step of The QPH Method, is therefore to apply the law of polarity, and begin to see and focus on the <u>HAVING</u> the outcome that you want, and not <u>WANTING</u>.

This is the power of Gratitude that is written throughout all religions. The power of Gratitude that is described in many self-help books.

Stating, that when you begin to focus on what you already have – you will begin to have more of it. That when you have enough, **life will bless you with even more.**

And by now when you've learned the principles of the mind – you can see how that works.

The problem then that we are left with is - <u>how do you control and direct your focus to see yourself having what you want?</u>

How to Plant New Seeds?

Another thing that is carefully hidden within books of religion including The Bible and Quran, is the god given gift – **ask, and you shall receive.**

The power of question is well understood in Entrepreneurship, business and many self-help exercises. But because people don't see how their experience is being created, and what asking a question really does, they miss the greatest gift god gave a human being – **an ability to get anything he wants.**

When you ask a question, your mind finds an answer. If you ask yourself, what is your favourite ice-cream, you will find the answer to the question you were asking for.

Up until you've asked that question, *you weren't even thinking about ice cream flavours.*

It is because questions direct your mind and your focus, the same way your beliefs direct your focus through Reticular Activation System.

Not only that, when you continue to ask, your mind will find answers – *even if they're not there.*

For example – if you think and feel bad about yourself, and you begin to ask question which implies that you are strong and confident, like *'How confident am I?'*, your mind will begin to look for experiences, where you are confident.

The question already implies, that you **HAVE IT.**

And when you gain control of your Reticular Activation System, and direct it to find examples and experiences where you are confident – you begin to see how your posture was good, how the tone of your voice was strong enough, how you express yourself, how other person reacted to you positively.

Naturally our beliefs -> focus our mind -> to find experiences that prove -> our beliefs are real.

When you ask a question, what you're doing is you're flipping this whole mechanism and instead you're searching for experiences yourself –> **to create a new belief.**

And by the law of polarity – <u>the opposite belief, ceases to exist.</u>

So, when you ask a question in your mind 'how confident am I?' your mind finds answers. Every time you see and get these answers in your mind – you get feelings and experience of what you perceive. The good feelings.

This is why positive thinking doesn't work, because thoughts leave as quickly as they come in, barely creating any feelings and when every thought is different – you can't produce real and permanent change. The same is with affirmations and visualization. They lack the energy in the body in order to create – **a reference experience.**

Beliefs need proof. Every answer to a question directs your focus – <u>to see that proof.</u> Which over time accumulates into replacing the opposite belief with a new one. And new habits of thought begin to travel through the neurons of your brain.

This is why asking questions guarantees to build a belief. You control your focus and the RAS to find what you look for. And because you ask the same question, this is what happens:

1. Your mind looks for **specific** examples to support <u>one belief.</u>
2. After you make it a habit, it *continues asking the question in your subconscious mind* and *looking for examples* – just like belief do.

This is the key to the 3rd piece of The QP**H** Method.

How to Make New Seeds Grow?

The only way to eliminate old beliefs and associations, is to change them with the new, opposing ones.

In order to make real transformation, you have to do it over and over until those thoughts, <u>become habit of thought.</u>

A belief.

This is the easy part, because all you have to do is ask the same type of question, enough times, every single day <u>for 30 days</u> – until it becomes a subconscious process. Until your mind does it on autopilot and you don't even have to consider doing it.

So, let's do a quick run through with what you have to do in order to change things and what possible applications there are.

Step 1 – Awareness

Remember, the most important part of the process is to practice the SKILL of self-awareness. Observing your thoughts and your experiences.

Because only when you can draw connections between how your mind is leading you into the experiences that you're having, only then you will begin to find your own answers to <u>where the problems lie.</u>

And then, you will be able to change them once and for all.

So, how do you practice self-awareness?

I recommend that from day 1 you would put your best effort to simply **self-observe** and catch each and every thought that comes into your mind.

When you have things happening outside, when you are made to feel worse, react or something more intense happened, simply stop and look inside - *what are you thinking?*

Ask questions what do I think about this? Why am I feeling this way? <u>Direct the focus</u> of your mind inward.

Once you start this process you should aim to commit to practice it as much as you can for the first 30 days – because after that, you will have acquired a skill.

A habit of self-observation, which will lead you to self-discovery. A skill that philosophers cultivated as their greatest power and path to understand themselves and the world around them.

As an alternative, if you find time, energy and have desire to do this work properly and with all of your intention – you can **write down questions** - to explore your thinking, your feelings, of the situations that bother you. As a daily exercise – focusing on the present moment.

Try and connect them to your past experiences. Associations of pain and pleasure. Your beliefs.

This is very powerful, because it's like a domino effect, where after the first question and the first answer you go down the rabbit hole until you begin to find your own answers and connections.

This was how I was able to Pioneer the QPH Method, a new

ability to change beliefs. And this is how I was able to draw connections from different beliefs to every single problem we could ever experience in our lives – individually and even at a society level.

The QPH Method – 3 Steps

In order to apply The QPH Method and change your beliefs, first you have to know **what do you WANT?**

What you want in terms of wanting something and realizing that you keep getting the opposite. For example, knowing that you want to be happy, but finding yourself unhappy.

OR, knowing how you want to feel about a certain aspect of your life. For example, you want to quit drinking, so you would like to associate pain with the act of drinking, so that you would naturally move away from it and never drink again.

You have two types of beliefs – **identity beliefs** and **beliefs about the world.**

When you want to change beliefs about yourself and your identity, you have to assume the positive qualities you want to have and ask question so that your mind would begin to see you that way.

For example, if I asked a question of 'How funny am I?', it would begin to look how funny am I in different situations. The presumption of HOW, intensity, already looks for the highest positive answer.

When you want to change beliefs about the world, you have to <u>change the emotional association to the perception of that thing.</u>

For example, if I want to stop playing computer games, I will have to change the association in my mind and link it to pain, so that I would naturally stop doing it. I would then ask a question *'how painful does it feel when I play computer games?'.*

Applying The QPH Method is literally as easy as thinking and won't even take 2-minutes out of your day. This is the beauty of it.

So, let's quickly recap:

The first step: Find out what you want to HAVE. You have to make sure you apply the law of polarity. If it's something you don't have yet – <u>assume you have it.</u> If it's something you're not – <u>assume you already are.</u>

The second step: Turn it into a simple question. Ether *'how strong am I?'* or *'how good does it feel when I eat cake?'* or *'how okay does it feel to be rejected?'.* Our minds don't understand complex language.

Even when we are little, our minds think the same way we do '<u>It feels painful</u> *when* **I steal**', or 'it is bad when I don't listen'.

So, we construct our questions the same way, but the goal is to change something we don't want into something we want. So, the change is prominent. So that we get what we want. So that we create what we WANT.

Step 3: Ask that question in your mind or read it every day in your notes in your phone, <u>for 30 days.</u> The more frequently you do it throughout the day – the more you train your mind to find more examples, making belief stronger, building it faster and creating a habit where it will continue to grow <u>at a faster rate.</u>

If you have a big problem you want to solve, do it intensely. If it's something you simply want to acquire – read it once <u>right before bed</u>, before setting your alarm and going to bed. This way, you leverage the mind, where that question, and answer spirals into thinking about it and finding reference examples as you sleep.

And if you do it <u>first thing in the morning</u>, - you will often find that throughout the day the answers pop into your mind. Because what you did was set the direction of your mind to go, at the very beginning of your day.

Typically, you won't spend any more than 2-minutes. When you write down a couple of questions in your notes or ask within your mind, it will be the easiest thing you've ever done.

The difficulty comes from valuing and <u>remembering to ask the questions</u> in the first place. This is why I recommend you **use your notes, and create a new habit** of doing this inner work, every time before you set your alarm and place your phone down before sleep; and first thing after waking up.

What should you expect?

The key to seeing change and transformation lies in your ability <u>to see how your experience is being created.</u>

When you see your thoughts and how they lead to your feelings – and you change them, only then you can see how powerful this transformation truly is.

On top of that, when you are self-aware, you will easily catch the thoughts that come in as you ask your questions. Seeing them, experiencing them and vividly creating change.

A person who is not self-aware will not notice the change – because he is not aware of his experience.

When life is outside, we are in constant motion of responding and getting distracted by what's going on. Our thoughts and feelings quickly move us to the next thought, feeling and action to take. The whole process is automatic.

When you can't see how you're steering the wheel and all you see is the road ahead, when you physically turn the wheel to the side, you won't see the connection between the wheel being turned and the change in direction – you'll still only see the road ahead.

Another aspect is the influence of our physical health.

When you have more sensitive biology, you are far more in tune with your thoughts and experience. You experience everything more intensely, you build memories and beliefs faster. You notice more and you are far more in tune even with the little things.

This is why by nature women are better at this. This is why by nature women can see and experience this far easier than a man would. We have different biology.

However, the foods we eat, highly affect our levels of sensitivity and hormone balance within the body. Your age is also at play with the natural ability to create hormones. What kind of foods do you eat and in what amounts.

If you're a man you can leverage plant foods, spices, herbs and drinks like green tea as most plant foods have sensitizing biology, healing qualities which act by making the body more sensitive. Also, this is how plants are able to absorb the nutrients from the soil, sun, water and oxygen from outside-in.

But beware, too much sensitivity is <u>not good.</u> Because if you use up too much energy or you become too stressed the body begins to preserve itself and slow down in order to survive. And a slow body creates all kinds of problems, from inability to produce energy, digesting food, absorbing it, creating energy and many others.

As you begin to ask the questions you will notice your thoughts and emotions change from the moment you ask the questions. You will be able to experience transformation from day 1. But it is consistency and building them up that will bring the greatest transformation.

Within the first week – it is easy to notice the answers. You see many examples. You notice the change from where you were to where you are going vividly.

Within the second week – you notice everything less. Often, you'll notice examples pop into your mind on their own. The process slowly begins to <u>take place on its own.</u> You may need a little more effort to make sure you get the answers.

Within the third week – it's easier to ask the question and the answers feel like second nature to you. You get them so easily that you might not even notice them coming in. If you rely on asking the question from your intention – you may begin to feel that you're forgetting to ask the question, where in reality – <u>*it's slowly becoming subconscious.*</u>

This is where you want to ensure that transformation is complete, and put in all the effort, to make sure that you come through.

The two mistakes you want to avoid

These are the mistakes that I've found my students are were most likely to make at the beginning:

Changing the questions you ask – people can often misinterpret the main point of the method. Which is to ask the same exact, specific question, in the same exact wording and form, <u>without changing it.</u>

In the early days, I've found that my students would ask questions as a *positive way to change their thinking.* Which will be effective indeed. But it won't bring a specific and permanent change, to where everything in your life would begin to change.

This is the power of this method over any other method – you can create REAL, and PERMANENT transformation. A complete fix of the problem, at the very core of where it was created. And once you eliminate it – <u>it is forever gone.</u> Once you create a powerful self-image – <u>it is forever there with you, wherever you go.</u>

This is the most powerful ability you could ever have – an ability written within the Bible and Quran. That **you can have what you want.** You can choose 100% of your experience in life.

So it is of upmost importance that you ask the same exact question over and over again. Because otherwise it won't become a habit and you won't receive the change you initially desire.

Rushing through the question – another big mistake I've found in the early days of developing this method, was that people asked the question, <u>to ask the question.</u>

You see, the power of the method does not lie in asking the question. **It lies in receiving the answer.**

If you ask the question and don't wait, don't observe and don't expect to get an answer, you cannot get <u>a reference experience, which would support a positive belief.</u>

Without a reference example – your belief has no ground for it to be real. You need proof. What makes us believe in things is seeing proof, examples, references for our beliefs.

If you believe that people are against you, and someone said a bad word to you, you go 'aha, see, I told you people are evil'. The same way you reverse this, by asking 'how supportive of me are people?' you begin to notice them differently. Every thing you 'see' becomes a reference for that experience – which builds a new belief.

And you can't see people as evil, if in your mind – they're not. You know it. There's only place for one polar opposite.

Either you are strong or you're weak. Either you are a good basketball player or a bad basketball player. Maybe at <u>different intensities</u>, but **you can only focus on one side, or the other.**

Therefore, to make a transformation, you have to get answers. You have to see it in your mind. And create new beliefs, while erasing the old ones.

You have the power to choose the experiences you want to have over things that happened to you in the past without your choice. <u>And change how you feel about them.</u>

Chapter 3 - How to achieve freedom?

So how do you achieve freedom, calmness and presence in your life? How can you use The QPH Method in order to turn your life around?

In this chapter I will reveal to you what it takes to achieve real freedom from within.

But first, I want to share with you the most powerful experience you can have in your life.

An ability to calm your mind, accept the world around you, stop your mind wandering and travelling to the future or the past – **and place it into the present moment.**

Ability to be here and now. And to experience each moment without distraction, with more intensity, pleasure and awareness.

The Secret of Happiness & Presence

What I'm about to reveal to you I consider the greatest gift and the most powerful thing I was able to do using The QPH Method, even years after pioneering the method.

The first time I used The QPH Method, my life changed within days. Like a 180-degree turnaround, I went from a life of depression into having complete confidence everywhere I went.

This transformation was so lucrative, of how quick it was and how powerful it was, that I decided to try it again with a different question.

At the time, I've recently read a book 'The Power of Now' by Eckhart Tolle. The idea of the book and being in the present moment seemed realistic, but also mystical to some degree.

I wasn't into spirituality, so I thought *'If this method works with something like this, then it must really be something extraordinary that I've discovered'.*

After I've applied The QPH Method to this idea, I began to notice very quick changes in my experience.

At the time I recently graduated Sports Medicine in University of Aberdeen and still lived there, in Scotland. As I was walking down Union Street, the main street I began to notice:

Every time I ask this question – **my awareness broadens.** I see more of everything. I begin to see everything happening at once – and there's this really pleasant feeling that comes with it. *Almost like some superpower.*

Every time I ask it, I really enjoy the feeling. So, I keep doing it more and more.

Within about a week something strange happened. I was taking a bus to work and sat down in front by the window. As I'm riding the bus, I've noticed another change in experience...

For the whole trip on the bus, I'm looking through the window, and I see simple things happening all around me, like women walking with a trolley, or a boy running towards his family. All of this time, my mind was entirely and fully present in these moments.

And it hit me...

What I found strange, was that my mind stopped thinking about things that might happen at work... things that happened yesterday... things I need to buy tonight when I go to a supermarket...

<u>They were entirely gone… and replaced by these experiences of things happening around me.</u>

At the time, that was all I've noticed. But as the years passed by, I've noticed many more changes from this one powerful question.

Because my mind stopped travelling to the future or the past, I've found that once the day is over, I don't think about it. What I mean is I found it hard to remember things of the past. If someone asked me something – I could still remember, but if I had to think about what happened on my own, I would have to put in some thought to it.

The next thing that changed – **was me…**

I was different than I used to be… But <u>not in a way that anyone could tell.</u> I was more at peace. I was happier.

I noticed that I entirely stopped resisting the moments – *that I have no control over.* I only began to notice this years later, that when other people get frustrated about things happening outside of them – In the same moments where in the past I would get emotional as well, <u>I felt calm and at peace.</u>

I was accepting of things for how they were. I was more accepting of people – of the way they are.

This is what I call **the question of Happiness and Presence.** What once felt like a lucrative idea, became a true gift of life. And I have to thank Eckhart Tolle for his work in this field as well.

Because combining our knowledge and discoveries can now give you the power to <u>PRACTICALLY</u> achieve what people think is *'spiritual'* or simply a *'wonderful idea'*.

What you're about to discover is what people spend their entire lives looking for it. I've met millionaires ready to pay $100,000 to help them deal with inability to find time for their family and peace within. Other people buy tickets to Asia to travel and live with the monks for several years, just so they could acquire the ever-lasting piece and unity in their lives.

While other people live their whole lives in suffering, whether affected by war, poverty, famine and unfortunate circumstances of life, OR having everything and still suffering in the privacy of their mind.

You have an opportunity to achieve the improbable, without even meditating and in a matter of days – **and make it last your whole lifetime.**

There is no greater gift than that.

So how do YOU do it?

The secret of it lies in control.

Remember - desire makes us see what we don't have. And fear makes us want for the present moment to be different the way it is.

Pain and fear, that desire for something to be different, creates **the need for control**. We want to change what is happening outside of us but comes from inside.

The self-created suffering, from an illusion within our minds. Which appears REAL only to us.

But the reality of life is that the only thing that you have control over – **is your mind.** You can't change the weather, you can't control other people, you can't control what will happen to you...

You can be having a walk outside and a car can hit you and *it might not even be your fault*... <u>you have no control over what will happen to you.</u>

The only thing you have control over is **your mind.** While most people are aware that they have *conscious control*, my gift to you is to give you an ability and awareness of <u>*subconscious control.*</u>

So, because you can't control what is happening, means you can't control the present moment. Resistance means trying to control (resist) the present moment.

But when you accept the present moment, the way that it is – *all need for control disappears*. You are free from feeling resistance, pain and fear to things that are happening outside of you.

You have to ACCEPT what you HAVE.

And let go of trying to control it. *(This is what most people say, without a practical way to do it. But I will show you how to practically do this.)*

Instead of focusing on what you **WANT this moment** – you must focus on:

  'What do I <u>have</u> this moment?' *– The question of total acceptance and constant focus on the present moment, which is a gift of life.*

When you begin to ask this question, you will begin to eliminate wanting for things to be different than the way they are.

Instead, you will begin to focus solely on the moments happening <u>right now</u>. And you will focus on the things you have right now. Which is **'the present moment'**. <u>The gift, given to you by life</u>.

And when your focus broadens – you will begin to get even more of <u>what you believe you have</u>. Making you always accept *'what is'*, and feel good, about **what you already have.**

Not All beliefs are created equally.

While I have revealed the most powerful and most liberating question of all I want to give you a heads-up of what it takes, to achieve <u>complete freedom in our lives.</u>

While the belief of presence and happiness is amazing to have, it will NOT eliminate the associations and fear-based beliefs from our minds.

You see we have different kinds of beliefs. We have beliefs about who we are. We have beliefs about what feels good and what feels bad in life. We have beliefs about what we believe to be good or bad.

But the key to understanding the biggest barriers, the biggest struggle, pain and fear in life, lies in the fact that **not all beliefs are created equally.**

We have beliefs that we are creating right now, with every new experience AND we have beliefs that start at the very roots, at the very beginning of our lives and at the very CORE of survival and reproduction.

Meaning they have are like the first domino pieces, pre-determining every belief that was ever built on top. And they have the strongest roots.

These are what I call – **Core Beliefs.** And there's something even more powerful about these core beliefs.

Potential Association Principle

This principle highlights why often **one single belief** – can act like <u>the greatest barrier in life.</u>

Think of it like this:

If you eat a pizza and you have the most horrible experience you've ever had. This experience becomes a memory of how painful it feels to eat pizza. And now you can't have pizza anymore.

<u>How often</u> can you experience this belief becoming real?

Maybe you'll see your friend order it and you will remember what it's like. That belief coming back into your reality and you re-experiencing it. But in reality – *<u>not in a way where it would prevent you from living your life right?</u>*

Now, let's take a look at one of the most acknowledged and well-aware beliefs that we all commonly have – **the fear of rejection.**

Most people are aware it exists, because most of us have experienced it in multiple areas of our lives.

But it also has a way of being re-experienced, without being noticed. This is where Potential Association Principle comes into play.

Our minds are very good at predicting danger, in order to help us <u>survive</u>. What they do, they are capable of predicting the POTENTIAL of experiencing pain and fear – danger.

When the mind perceives the potential of experiencing danger, it moves away from it. It becomes an **<u>invisible barrier.</u>**

For example, when a student reads his work in front of class, he begins to feel anxiety, stress and worry. Most people would call this 'fear of public speaking'. But in reality – there's a POTENTIAL that he will experience ***the fear of rejection.***

If he says something wrong and people laugh = *potential for rejection.*

If he gets a bad grade, comes home and his parents get angry = *potential for rejection.*

If his friends turn against him = *potential for rejection.*

Now the more he wants to avoid this, the more likely he is to make that mistake, which will lead to others laughing, or getting a worse grade = re-experiencing the feeling of rejection *(belief becoming reality).*

When a guy goes over to a girl, whether **he fails** OR whether he **succeeds, and then loses her** = *both have potential of re-experiencing rejection.*

This is what people call the 'fear of failure' and 'fear of success'. Because <u>there's a potential to fail after succeeding.</u>

The power of potential association principle is that these beliefs can be re-experiences in everything we do. They are not only the first beliefs that we get after birth, but also they are the strongest and most prominent beliefs to guide our lives and help us survive.

When you have a conversation and someone doesn't like you, when you apply for a new job, when you win a lottery and people might turn against you. They can be re-experienced in multiple ordinary experiences, creating worries, hesitations, barriers <u>in the little things in life.</u>

Now in order to explain them further and understand them, *it's a whole different ball game.* If you want to learn more about them, I recommend you read 'The QPH Method' main book (not the Quick Guide) or visit <u>selfmasteracademy.com</u> to learn everything there is on how they work, what effects and consequences they have and <u>how to recondition them</u>.

The basic principle is that after reading this book - you already have an ability to deal with everything, <u>including these core beliefs.</u>

By being able to observe your experience and self-discover **you can find any problem, pain and weakness.** The more information you acquire on the subject of beliefs, the more you will find where they have an effect in your life. And what beliefs do what.

What I wanted to illustrate is that we live our lives based on the experiences and things that happened to us early in life. Sometimes we have no control over the things that can happen to us. It may not be our fault, and it may not be our parents' fault – because they often raise us from how they were raised. Passing on beliefs and parenting from generation to generation.

While we have no conscious choice of how our lives will turn out – with discovering this book and The QPH Method, ability to change beliefs - you now have conscious choice over how your life will turn out from here. You can end the rat-race.

You can go back, change things in the moment – and change the whole course and future of your life. ***Your fate.***

There are an infinite number of beliefs that we have. Some are more powerful and more prominent than others. Others are powerful because we carry them everywhere with us (*our Identity beliefs*). Others dictate our motivations and desires (*associations*).

In order to create the life of your dreams you have to understand that **it's a process.**

It's a process of consciously unwiring the program in your mind that got created without your choice, so that it would begin to draw experiences in your life that you want to experience. So that you can eliminate certain feelings and create different ones.

You can unwire the beliefs from the bottom-up, and all beliefs on the top will begin to break and change on their own. And you can unwire beliefs from the top to bottom, in order to make changes from multiple directions and begin to see the little changes you want to see.

The biggest mistake I have made with The QPH Method, was that I used it once to create Confidence to escape the life of depression and then acquired Happiness and Presence belief – *and put the method behind me.*

Because in years to come, I had to find out why I was still experiencing feelings of jealousy in my relationship, and it had to come to an end. Why was I still experiencing barriers from achieving my dream career and why I still had not created my dream life.

Only 18 years later, after I re-experienced the pain of losing my dad (at the age of 6), I've realized, that the work was not yet done.

I've realized that if I wanted to have a different relationship, where it doesn't follow the same course – I would have more work to do.

And after finding all my barriers, and changing them, was when I became free of those little habits, feelings and actions that would influence my relationships. The path of least resistance to succeed opened up at my feet. And that was when I was able to achieve <u>total freedom and the ability to be happy regardless of what I had.</u>

It's a process.

It's your opportunity to have a different life.

If you've enjoyed this book, please consider leaving a positive review and let us know how valuable you found this book.

All the best,

Vytas Kas.

About Vytas Kas

Vytas Kas is an established Author, Professional Consultant, Pioneer and developer of The QPH Method - a new human ability to change human beliefs and associations within the subconscious mind.

He is world's leading expert, specializing in human mind and belief reprogramming, through practical methodology and principles.

His work greatly contributes to the Science of Psychology, Philosophy, Business & Marketing and Medical Sciences. In 2015, University of Aberdeen, Scotland, Vytas was awarded with a diploma in Sports Medicine, in which he studied Advanced Psychology, Medical Sciences and Coaching.

Vytas findings provide a practical method for Psychologists and Practitioners all over the world, to effectively deal with psychological transformation.

He is a mentor and a hero to people who suffer from Psychologically induced mental health conditions, procrastination, relationship problems, personal barriers, trauma, negative self-image, anxiety and other problems affecting one's personal quality of life, experience and achievement.

For more, please visit vytas-kas.com.

Recommended Resources for Further Development:

Self-Master Academy - The only place where you can self-educate, master your ability to change beliefs, and receive help and support. Discover different beliefs and their impact in your life, so you can gain conscious control of your life, strengthen your confidence, build courage, improve your relationships and achieve your dream life faster than ever before.

✓ **Core-Beliefs & Their Reconditioning**

✓ **Discovery of Most Powerful & Impactful Beliefs**

✓ **How to Accelerate Belief Transformation**

✓ **Energy Flow Beliefs (7 Chakra's)**

✓ **Valuable Resources**

✓ **Ask Questions & Get Support**

Join the vast community of Freedom Academy, people who are transforming their lives by reprogramming their beliefs.

For more please visit *selfmasteracademy.com*

Recommended Reading:

The QPH Method: Gain Control of Your Beliefs, Emotions & Success in Life – at The Speed of Thought

(Full Book, by Vytas Kas)

amazon   BARNES&NOBLE   Apple Books.   Rakuten kobo   ///bibliotheca